The
Oxford Picture Dictionary
for Kids

Joan Ross Keyes

Illustrated by Sally Springer

OXFORD UNIVERSITY PRESS

OXFORD
UNIVERSITY PRESS

198 Madison Avenue
New York, NY 10016 USA

Great Clarendon Street
Oxford OX2 6DP England

Oxford New York

Auckland Cape Town Dar es Salaam Hong Kong Karachi
Kuala Lumpur Madrid Melbourne Mexico City Nairobi
New Delhi Shanghai Taipei Toronto

With offices in

Argentina Austria Brazil Chile Czech Republic France Greece
Guatemala Hungary Italy Japan Poland Portugal Singapore
South Korea Switzerland Thailand Turkey Ukraine Vietnam

OXFORD is a trademark of Oxford University Press.

ISBN: 978 0 19 434996 3 (hardcover)

ISBN: 978 0 19 434997 0 (softcover)

Editor Manager: Shelagh Speers
Senior Editor: June Schwartz
Editor: Dorothy Bukantz
Production Editor: M. Long
Elementary Design Manager: Doris Chen
Art Buyer: Donna Goldberg
Production Manager: Abram Hall

Printing (last digit): 20 19 18 17 16 15 14

Printed in Hong Kong.

Cover illustration by Sally Springer
Illustrations by Sally Springer
Cover design by Doris Chen

Additional art by: Gary Torrisi; Robert Frank/Melissa Turk & The Artist Network; Marcia
Hartsock, CMI; Elizabeth Wolf/Melissa Turk & The Artist Network; Andrea Tacheira;
Stephen Nicodemus; and John Paul Genzo.

Acknowledgements

To all my students everywhere whose appreciation and enthusiasm motivated me to create
this book, its stories, dialogues, and Beats!

To the special people at Oxford University Press: the design and production staff for
ingeniously putting all the parts together, to Shelagh Speers, the Editorial Manager, for her
"go for it" encouragement, and most of all to my own editor, June Schwartz, whose patient
labors got us through it all.

And to my family, my daughter and three sons, for understanding and giving me space . . .

I thank you all.

JRK

Preface

The Oxford Picture Dictionary for Kids is designed especially for young students, ages five to seven, who are learning English.

The dictionary presents over 700 words in the context of pictures that tell stories. Five characters and their families are introduced at the beginning of the book, and appear throughout in 60 double-page illustrations.

Dictionary Organization

Each double-page illustration introduces a topic. The 60 topics are organized into nine themes. The initial focus is on the individual characters' experiences within the family, at home, and at school. The focus then expands to include their experiences in the neighborhood, around the town, and in other environments in the United States and around the world. Although the topics follow a logical progression, each topic is self-contained so that they may be presented to students in any order.

Under the double-page illustration in each topic are words and pictures corresponding to the objects or actions shown in that illustration. Each word is accompanied by a small picture that duplicates the item in the larger illustration. These *callouts* define the words. They help children isolate each item and search for it in the context of the picture story.

Each topic has 12 numbered callouts. In addition to the callout vocabulary, some pages have labels, such as for rooms in the house and in the school. The number of words has been kept to a minimum so that students will be able to master the vocabulary more easily. Verbs and nouns are included in topics together to encourage students to use the language in context. Verbs are grouped together on the page. Each verb is marked with a star.

Appendix and Word Lists

Following the 60 topics is an appendix that includes the alphabet, numbers, colors, shapes, days, months, and time.

After the appendix are three lists: *Words, Verbs,* and *Subjects.* The *Words* list, arranged alphabetically, includes the callout nouns and verbs, labels, and key words from the titles. These are listed in black. Listed in red are additional words that do not appear in the text, but are pictured in the illustrations.

The *Verbs* list is arranged by the topics in which verbs can be found.

The *Subjects* list is a convenient cross-reference, by category, of words that can be found within several different topics and themes.

Using the Dictionary as a Program

The dictionary can be used by itself or with other components that make it suitable as the core of an entire English-language curriculum. These components include the *Teacher's Book, Reproducibles Collection, Workbook, Cassettes,* and *Wall Charts.*

The Reproducibles Collection is a boxed set of four books of reproducible pages: *Word and Picture Cards, Stories, Beats!,* and *Worksheets.* The *Stories* describe each illustration; the *Beats!* are playful rhythmic chants for each topic. In the *Stories* and *Beats!* books, each illustrated sheet folds to make a mini-book for students to take home.

The *Teacher's Book,* in addition to complete notes for every topic, contains annotated bibliographies of appropriate theme-related literature to help create a classroom library.

The *Picture Dictionary* is available in both monolingual and bilingual editions.

Contents

Theme 4: My Town

Me

Tommy

Ting

Alison

Diego

Zoe

My family

The Matthews family

The Cheng family

The Young family

1.  sister

2. brother

3.  mother

4. father

5. parents

6. children

The Lopez family

The Jackson family

7. grandmother

8. grandfather

9.  aunt

10.  uncle

11. cousins

12. baby

Different faces

1. eyes

2. ears

3. nose

4. mouth

5. tooth / teeth

6. chin

7. eyelashes

8. skin

9. hair

10. straight

11. curly

12.  glasses

Big world!

North America

Atlantic Ocean

Pacific Ocean

South America

Europe

Asia

Africa

Australia

N
W E
S

Antarctica

Where do you live?

1. house

2. apartment

3. hill

4. street

5. address

6. telephone

7. window

8. door

9. roof

10. tree

11. yard

12. fence

Good morning!

bedroom

bathroom

living room

1. stove

2. table

3. sink

4. dresser

5. bed

6.  sofa

bedroom

kitchen

 7. cook

 8. eat

 9. wash

 10. brush

 11. get dressed

 12. sleep

Busy bathroom!

1. water

2. brush

3. comb

4. bathtub

5. shower

6. toothbrush

7. toothpaste

8. shampoo

9. soap

10. towel

11. toilet

12. toilet paper

What can I wear?

1. sweater

2. underwear

3. sneakers

4. socks

5. baseball cap

6. dress

7. skirt

8. sweatshirt

9. jeans

10. T-shirt

11. boots

12. pajamas

Who made breakfast?

1. bowl

2. plate

3. cup

4. glass

5. knife

6. fork

7. spoon

8. juice

9. butter

10. cereal

11. eggs

12. bread

Here comes the school bus!

1. bus stop

2. bus driver

3. corner

4. line

5.  seat

6. seat belt

7. lunch box

8. backpack

☆9. lean

☆10. push

☆11. stand

☆12. sit

Time for school

classroom

office

1. teacher

2. principal

3. nurse

4. student

5. crossing guard

6. librarian

library

art room

music room

nurse's office

cafeteria

gym

7. car

8. bicycle

9.  bus

10. clock

☆11. walk

☆12. ride

1.  picture

2. markers

3. pencil

4.  crayons

5. scissors

6. glue

7. blocks

☆8. build

☆9. listen

☆10. look

☆11. paint

☆12.  cut

Where's my homework?

Homework
Write a story.
Draw a picture.

1. book

2. notebook

3. paper

4. board

5. desk

6. chair

7.  chalk

8. wastebasket

☆9. write

☆10. draw

☆11. read

☆12. think

Bodies and bones!

1. head

2. neck

3. chest

4. stomach

5. back

6. buttocks

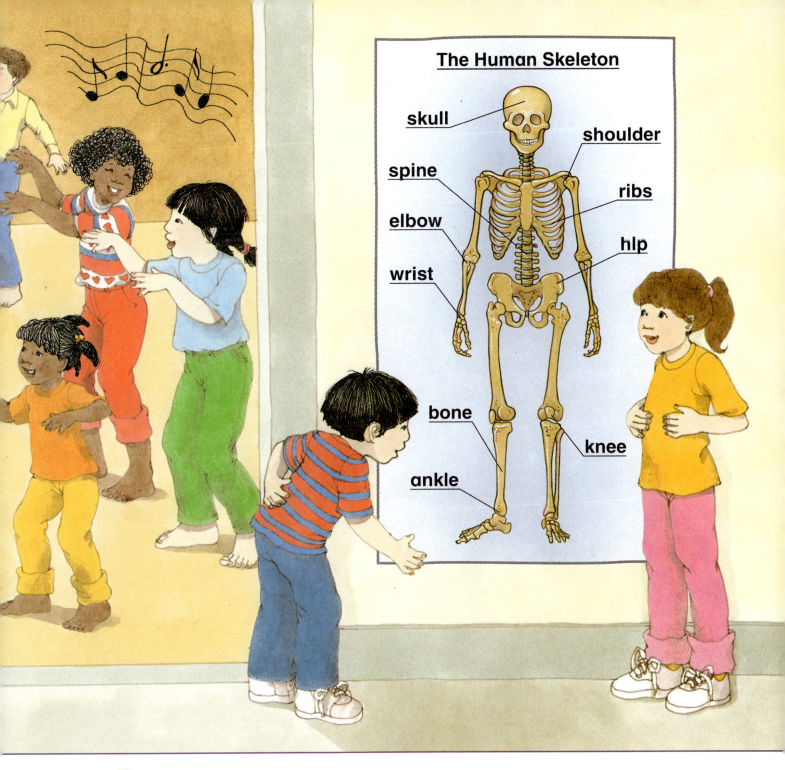

The Human Skeleton

skull

shoulder

spine

ribs

elbow

hlp

wrist

bone

knee

ankle

7. leg

8. foot / feet

9. toes

10.  arm

11. hand

12. fingers

What's new in the hall?

1. happy

2. sad

3. tired

4. surprised

5. angry

6. scared

7. worried

☆8. smile

☆9. yawn

☆10. cry

☆11. frown

☆12. laugh

Gym time!

1. hoop

2. around

3. between

4. over

5. through

6. under

7.  mat

☆8. skip

☆9. hop

☆10. crawl

☆11. jump

☆12.  tumble

What's for lunch?

1. tray

2. taco

3. apple

4. milk

5. can

6. carrot

7.  egg roll

8.  sushi

9. garbage can

10. sandwich

11. salad

12. cookie

Let's play!

1. swing

2. slide

3. bars

4. seesaw

5. ball

☆6. climb

☆7. throw

☆8. catch

☆9. bounce

☆10. fall

☆11.  run

☆12.  kick

What's the matter?

1.  stomachache

2. tissues

3. sore throat

4. fever

5. thermometer

6. bandage

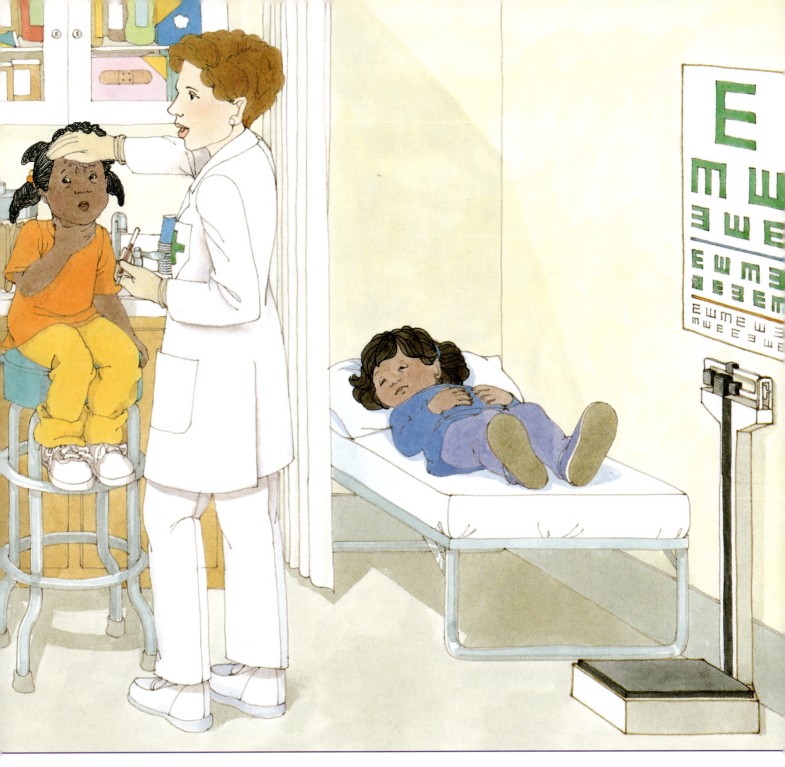

7. blood

8. cut

9. bump

☆10. cough

☆11. sneeze

☆12. lie down

Music!

1. violin

2. trumpet

3. tuba

4. flute

5. maracas

6. piano

7. 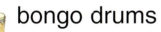 bongo drums

8. triangle

☆9. blow

☆10. beat

☆11. clap

☆12.  sing

1. police officer

2. traffic

3. traffic light

4. truck

5. motorcycle

6.  taxi

7. police station

8.  library

9.  sports store

10.  pet shop

11.  barbershop

12.  toy store

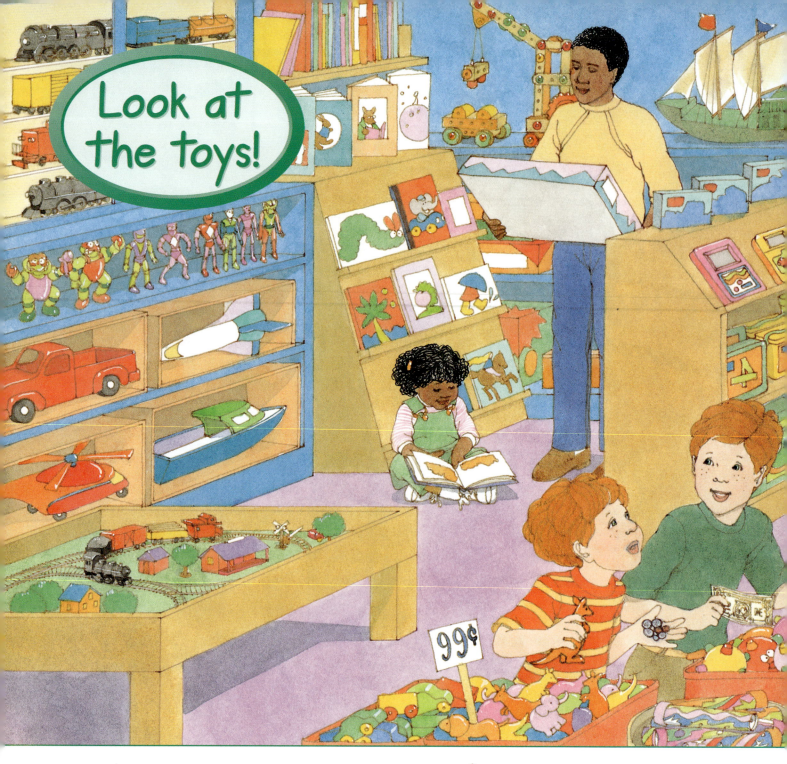

Look at the toys!

1. game

2.  airplane

3. boat

4.  doll

5.  animals

6.  train

7. money

8. quarter

9. dime

10. nickel

11. penny

12. dollar

Can we have a pet?

1. bird

2. fish

3. fish tank

4. turtle

5. mouse

6. cage

7. dog

8. cat

9. kitten

10. puppy

11. collar

12. leash

Let's go to the library!

AUTHOR: KEYES, J.R.
TITLE: OUR EARTH
SUBJECT: EARTH SCIENCE
CALL NUMBER: 551K

1.  magazine

2. newspaper

3. atlas

4. dictionary

5. computer

6.  call number

7. videotape

8. bookshelves

9. library card

10. due date

☆11. check out

☆12. return

I'm sick!

examination room

1. doctor

2. patient

3. checkup

4. chart

5. scale

6. stethoscope

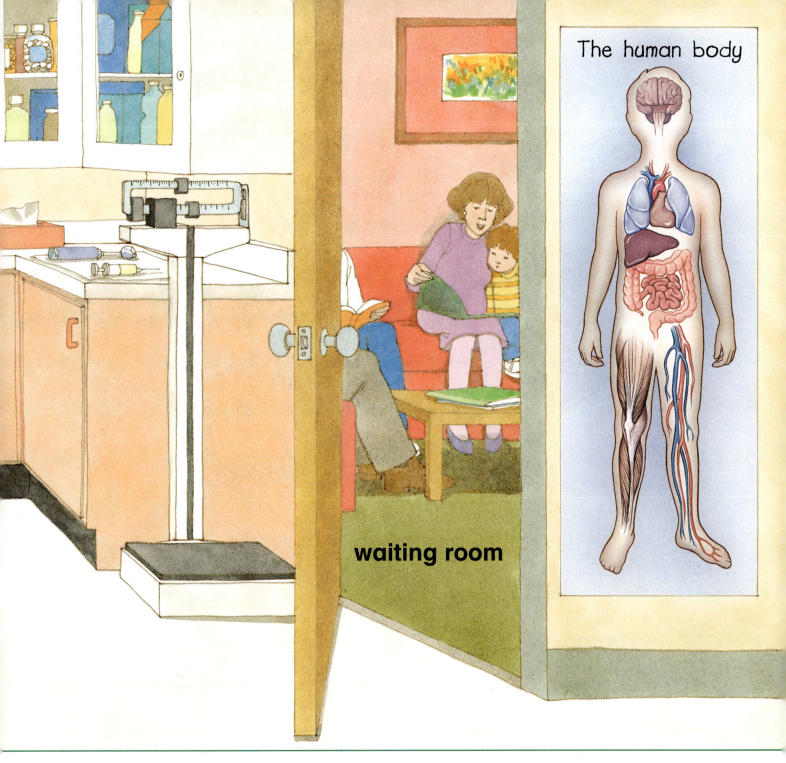

The human body

waiting room

7. medicine

8. drops

9. spray

10.  prescription

11. tablets

12. shot

Who's at the hospital?

nursery

waiting room

1. 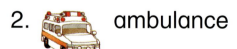 siren

2.  ambulance

3. paramedic

4. stretcher

5.  mask

6.  rubber gloves

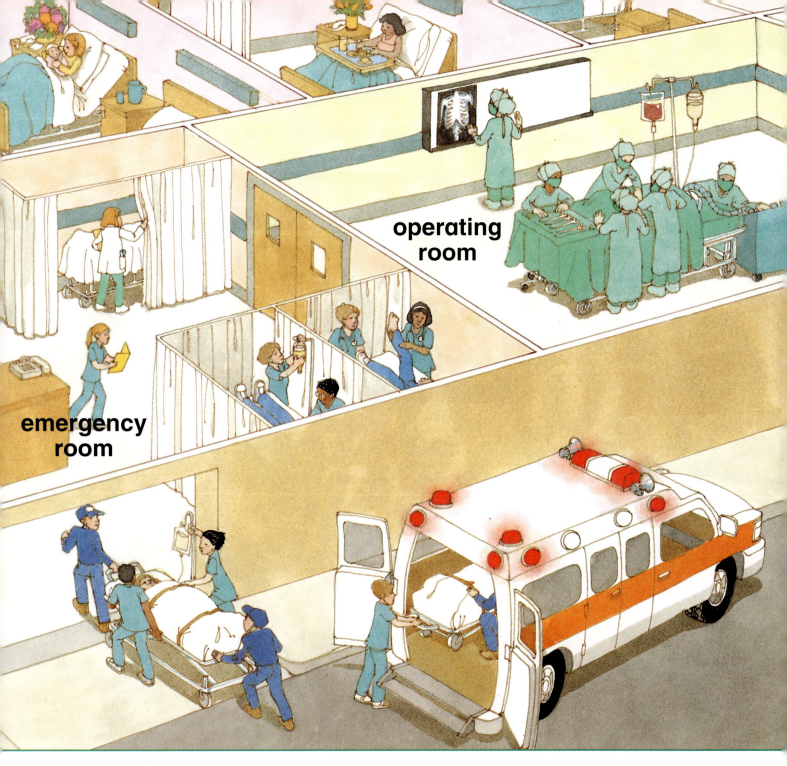

operating room

emergency room

7. X ray

8. wheelchair

9.  walker

10.  crutches

11. cast

12. blanket

Busy supermarket!

1.  list

2. pineapple

3. bananas

4. orange

5.  meat

6. seafood

7. box

8. bags

9. cart

10. lettuce

11. broccoli

12. cheese

Errands in town

1. restaurant

2. hardware store

3. drugstore

4. letter

5. letter carrier

6. mailbox

7. post office

8. dentist

9. laundry

10. bakery

11. bank

12. gas station

Dinner's ready!

1. roast beef

2. potato

3. peas

4. tomato

5. rolls

6. apple pie

7. soup

8. corn

9. chicken

10. rice

11. beans

12.  melon

Nice evening!

1. stereo

2. television

3.  remote

4. CD

5. headphones

6. radio

 ☆7. rest

 ☆8. play

 ☆9. watch

 ☆10. help

 ☆11. talk

 ☆12. practice

Saturday at the mall

1. movie theater

2. arcade

3. snack bar

4. pizza

5. french fries

6. ice cream cone

7. soda

8.  shoe store

9. 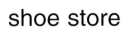 clothing store

10. rest rooms

11. escalator

12. exit

Happy birthday!

1. balloon

2.  present

3. card

4. ribbon

5. 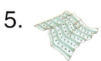 wrapping paper

6. baseball bat

January	February
S M T W T F S	S M T W T F S
1	1 2 3 4 5
2 3 4 5 6 7 8	6 7 8 9 10 11 12
9 10 11 12 13 14 15	13 14 15 16 17 18 19
16 17 18 19 20 21 22	20 21 22 23 24 25 26
23 24 25 26 27 28 29	27 28 29
30 31	

March	April
S M T W T F S	S M T W T F S
1 2 3 4	1
5 6 7 8 9 10 11	2 3 4 5 6 7 8
12 13 14 15 16 17 18	9 10 11 12 13 14 15
19 20 21 22 23 24 25	16 17 18 19 20 21 22
26 27 28 29 30 31	23 24 25 26 27 28 29
	30

May	June
S M T W T F S	S M T W T F S
1 2 3 4 5 6	1 2 3
7 8 9 10 11 12 13	4 5 6 7 8 9 10
14 15 16 17 18 19 20	11 12 13 14 15 16 17
21 22 23 24 25 26 27	18 19 20 21 22 23 24
28 29 30 31	25 26 27 28 29 30

July	August
S M T W T F S	S M T W T F S
1	1 2 3 4 5
2 3 4 5 6 7 8	6 7 8 9 10 11 12
9 10 11 12 13 14 15	13 14 15 16 17 18 19
16 17 18 19 20 21 22	20 21 22 23 24 25 26
23 24 25 26 27 28 29	27 28 29 30 31
30 31	

September	October
S M T W T F S	S M T W T F S
1 2	1 2 3 4 5 6 7
3 4 5 6 7 8 9	8 9 10 11 12 13 14
10 11 12 13 14 15 16	15 16 17 18 19 20 21
17 18 19 20 21 22 23	22 23 24 25 26 27 28
24 25 26 27 28 29 30	29 30 31

November	December
S M T W T F S	S M T W T F S
1 2 3 4	1 2
5 6 7 8 9 10 11	3 4 5 6 7 8 9
12 13 14 15 16 17 18	10 11 12 13 14 15 16
19 20 21 22 23 24 25	17 18 19 20 21 22 23
26 27 28 29 30	24 25 26 27 28 29 30
	31

7. jewelry

8. puzzle

9. helicopter

10. candy

11.  cake

12. candles

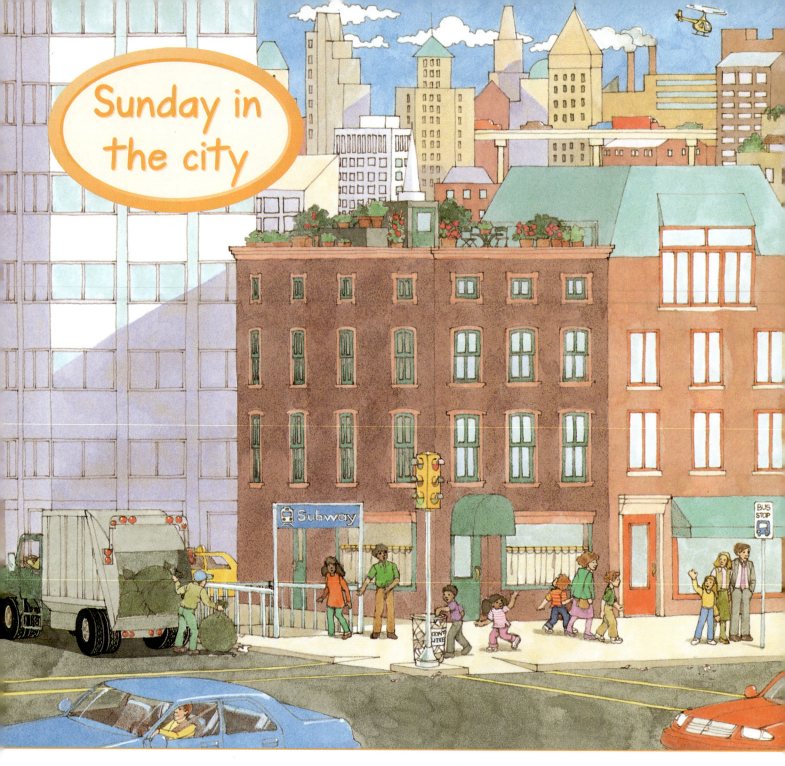

Sunday in the city

1. 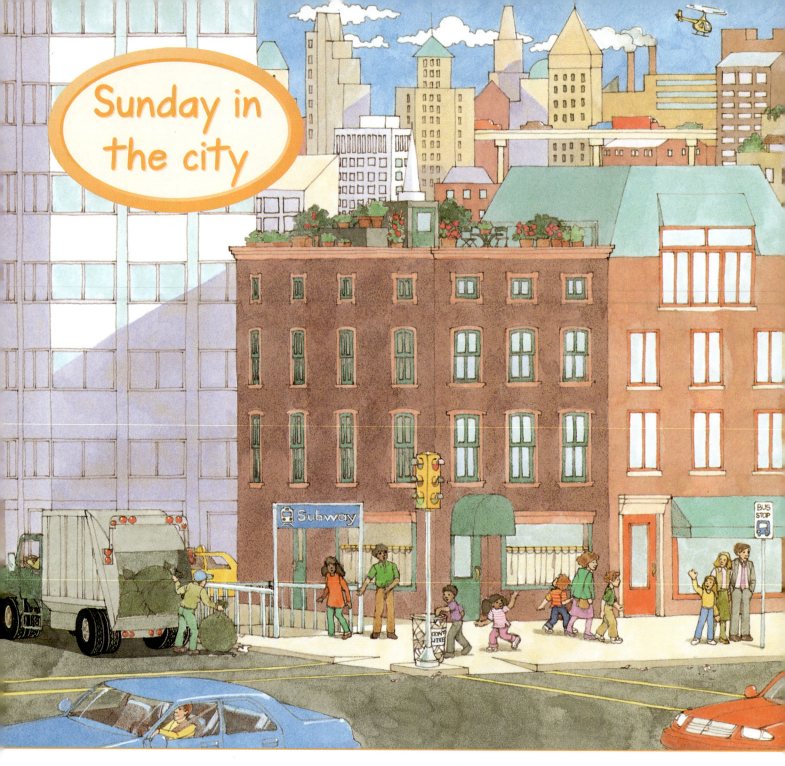 airport

2. railroad

3. highway

4. factory

5. smokestack

6. litter

7. street cleaner

8. garbage truck

9. skyscrapers

10. park

11. bench

12. subway

Street scene

1. singer

2. dancer

3. musician

4. guitar

5. photographer

6. camera

7. theater

8. museum

9.  steps

10. mime

11. artist

12. painting

New building going up!

1. backhoe

2.  dump truck

3. cement mixer

4. crane

5. forklift

6. bulldozer

7. construction worker

8. carpenter

9. plumber

10. electrician

11.  pipe

12. wire

Fire!

1. smoke

2. flame

3. fire engine

4. firefighter

5. fire chief

6. fire hydrant

fire safety

no matches

smoke detector

battery

call 911

7.  hose

8. axe

9. ladder

10. 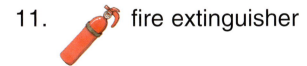 air tank

11. fire extinguisher

12. fire escape

Big harbor

1. sunset

2. lighthouse

3. ship

4. buoy

5. sailboat

6. bridge

7. ferry

8. dock

9. barge

10. warehouse

11. tugboat

12. anchor

Carnival!

1. ticket

2. popcorn

3. cotton candy

4. acrobat

5. trapeze

6. costume

7. magician

8. clown

9. Ferris wheel

10.  carousel

11.  puppet show

12.  fireworks

Great restaurant!

1.  tablecloth

2. napkin

3. apron

4. pots

5. chef

6. menu

7. chopsticks

8. waiter

☆9. pour

☆10. stir

☆11. chop

☆12.  serve

Let's see the USA!

1. desert

2. peninsula

3. mountains

4. lake

5. gulf

6. coast

7. forest

8. river

9. wetlands

10. plains

11. glacier

12. island

Beach day

1. seagull

2. sand

3. wave

4. sunburn

5. sunblock

6. lifeguard

7. surfboard

8. bathing suit

9. kite

☆10. swim

☆11. dive

☆12. float

We found a tide pool!

BIRD SANCTUARY
KEEP OUT

1. pail

2. shovel

3. stones

4. shells

5. clams

6. crabs

7. snail

8. minnows

9. seaweed

10. duck

11.  goose / geese

12.  pelican

What's under the sea?

1. dolphin

2. whale

3. spout

4. fins

5. snorkel

6.  school

7. coral reef

8. sea horse

9. shark

10. jellyfish

11. octopus

12. tentacles

Working on the farm

1. farmer

2. barn

3. tractor

4. cow

5. hen

6. rooster

7. sheep

8. pig

☆9.  drive

☆10. pick

☆11.  feed

☆12.  milk

Camping out

1. sunrise

2. waterfall

3. tent

4. sleeping bag

5. life jacket

6. rowboat

7. ![fishing rod] fishing rod

8. ![poison ivy] poison ivy

9. ![frog] frog

10. ![deer] deer

11. ![bear] bear

12. ![woods] woods

Bugs!

larva

eggs

pupa

adult

1. ant

2. spider

3. web

4. caterpillar

5. cocoon

6.  butterfly

7.  bee

8. ticks

9. firefly

10. mosquito

11. magnifying glass

12. bug spray

Ranch in the desert

1. cowhand

2. cactus

3. rattlesnake

4. coyote

5. prairie dog

6. lizard

7. horseback riding

8. rocks

9. lasso

10. buffalo

11. scorpion

12. horse

Dinosaur days

1. fossil

2. scientist

3.  dinosaurs

4. Oviraptor

5. Pterosaur

6. Triceratops

7. Stegosaurus

8. Tyrannosaurus Rex

9. Diplodocus

10. asteroid

11. volcano

12. lava

Who lives in the zoo?

1. peacock

2. monkeys

3.  elephant

4. tiger

5. lion

6. snakes

7.  ape

8. feathers

9. tail

10. trunk

11. scales

12. fur

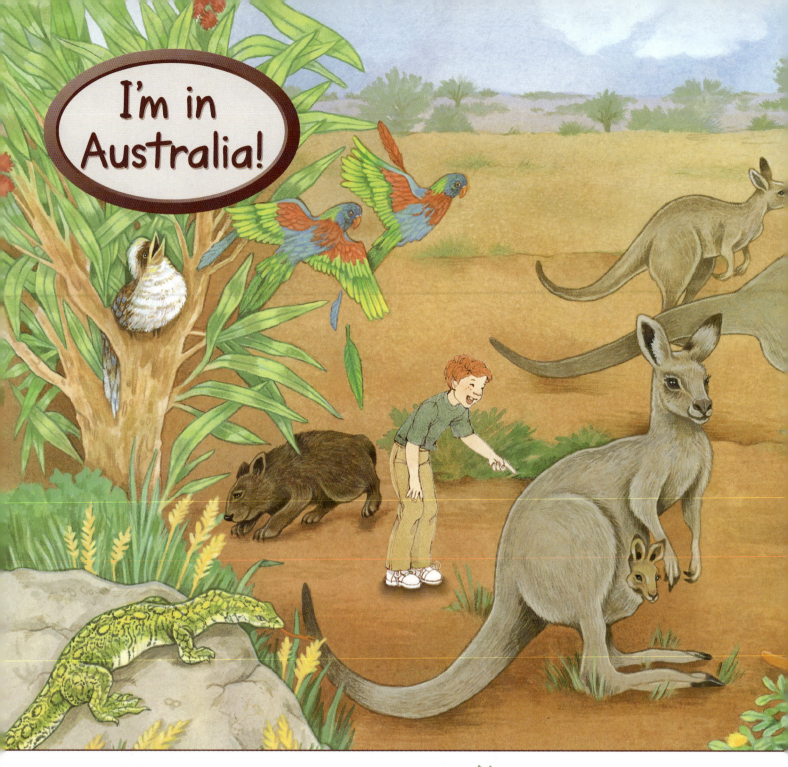

I'm in Australia!

1. emu

2. dingo

3. koala

4. kangaroo

5. joey

6. wichity grubs

7. wombat

8. kookaburra

9. parrot

10. claws

11. pouch

12. wings

I'm in Africa!

1. gazelle

2. hippopotamus

3. zebra

4. giraffe

5. gorilla

6. chimpanzee

7.  baboon

8. flamingo

9. leopard

10. jaws

11. spots

12. stripes

I'm in Asia!

1.  camel

2. orangutan

3. crocodile

4. cobra

5. rhinoceros

6. egret

7. panda

8. bamboo

9. humps

10. horn

11. beak

12. fangs

Spring is here!

1.  grass

2.  bush

3. flowers

4. lawn mower

5. rabbit

6. seeds

dig | plant | cover | water

7.  robin

8. nest

9. squirrel

10. raccoon

11. hammer

12. saw

We planted a garden!

Our Garden

Tomato

DAISY

Snapdragon

1. sunshine

2. rain

3. soil

4. seed

5. root

6. sprout

7. stem

8. leaf

9. bud

10. flower

11. raincoat

12. umbrella

Hot summer

1.  pool

2. baseball

3. tennis

4. waterskiing

5. skates

6. picnic

7. hamburger

8.  hot dog

9. clouds

10. wind

11. lightning

12. thunderstorm

Windy fall

1. leaves

2. rake

3. pile

4. wheelbarrow

5. clippers

6. broom

7. bulbs

8. football

9. soccer

10. pumpkin

11. woodpecker

12. nuts

Snowy winter

1. snow
2. snowflakes
3. snowman
4. snowball
5. icicles
6. sled

7.  ice skating

8.  skiing

9. hat

10.  jacket

11.  gloves

12.  scarf

Up in the night sky

1. moon

2. stars

3. constellation

4. meteor

5. comet

6. planets

7. astronomer

8. telescope

9.  full moon

10. half moon

11. crescent moon

12. new moon

Out in space

Saturn

Jupiter

Neptune

Uranus

Pluto

1.  The Sun

2. Mercury

3. Venus

4.  Earth

5. Mars

6.  Jupiter

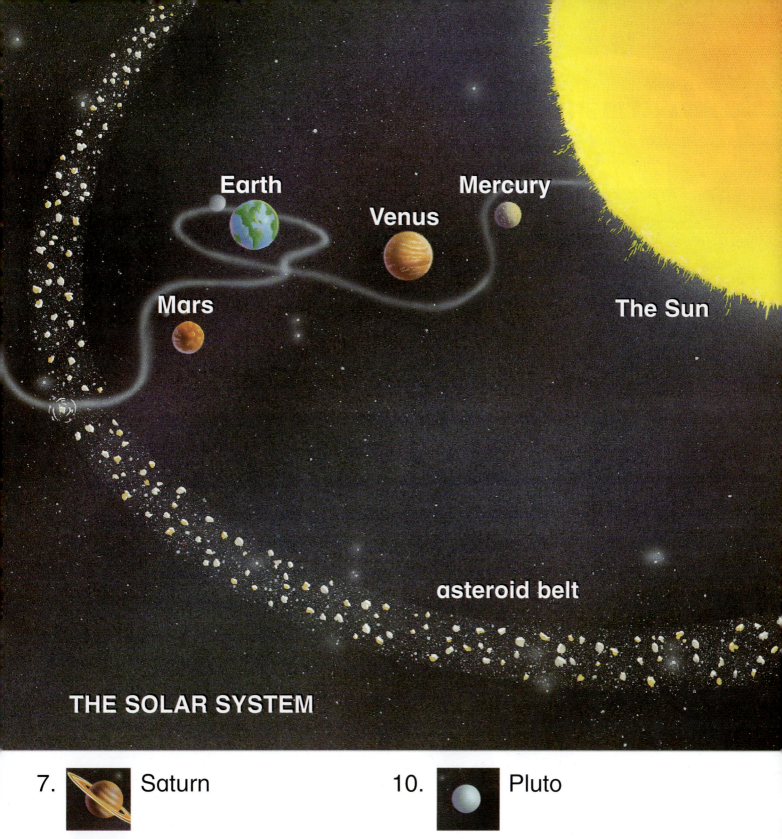

Earth

Mercury

Venus

Mars

The Sun

asteroid belt

THE SOLAR SYSTEM

7.  Saturn

8. Uranus

9.  Neptune

10. Pluto

11. astronaut

12. spaceship

Appendix

The Alphabet

A a   B b   C c

D d   E e   F f

G g   H h   I i

J j   K k   L l

M m   N n   O o

P p Q q R r

S s T t U u

V v W w X x

Y y Z z

Numbers

1	one	●
2	two	● ●
3	three	● ● ●
4	four	● ● ● ●
5	five	● ● ● ● ●
6	six	● ● ● ● ● ●
7	seven	● ● ● ● ● ● ●
8	eight	● ● ● ● ● ● ● ●
9	nine	● ● ● ● ● ● ● ● ●
10	ten	● ● ● ● ● ● ● ● ● ●
11	eleven	● ● ● ● ● ● ● ● ● ● ●
12	twelve	● ● ● ● ● ● ● ● ● ● ● ●
13	thirteen	● ● ● ● ● ● ● ● ● ● ● ● ●
14	fourteen	● ● ● ● ● ● ● ● ● ● ● ● ● ●
15	fifteen	● ● ● ● ● ● ● ● ● ● ● ● ● ● ●
16	sixteen	● ● ● ● ● ● ● ● ● ● ● ● ● ● ● ●
17	seventeen	● ● ● ● ● ● ● ● ● ● ● ● ● ● ● ● ●
18	eighteen	● ● ● ● ● ● ● ● ● ● ● ● ● ● ● ● ● ●
19	nineteen	● ● ● ● ● ● ● ● ● ● ● ● ● ● ● ● ● ● ●
20	twenty	● ● ● ● ● ● ● ● ● ● ● ● ● ● ● ● ● ● ● ●

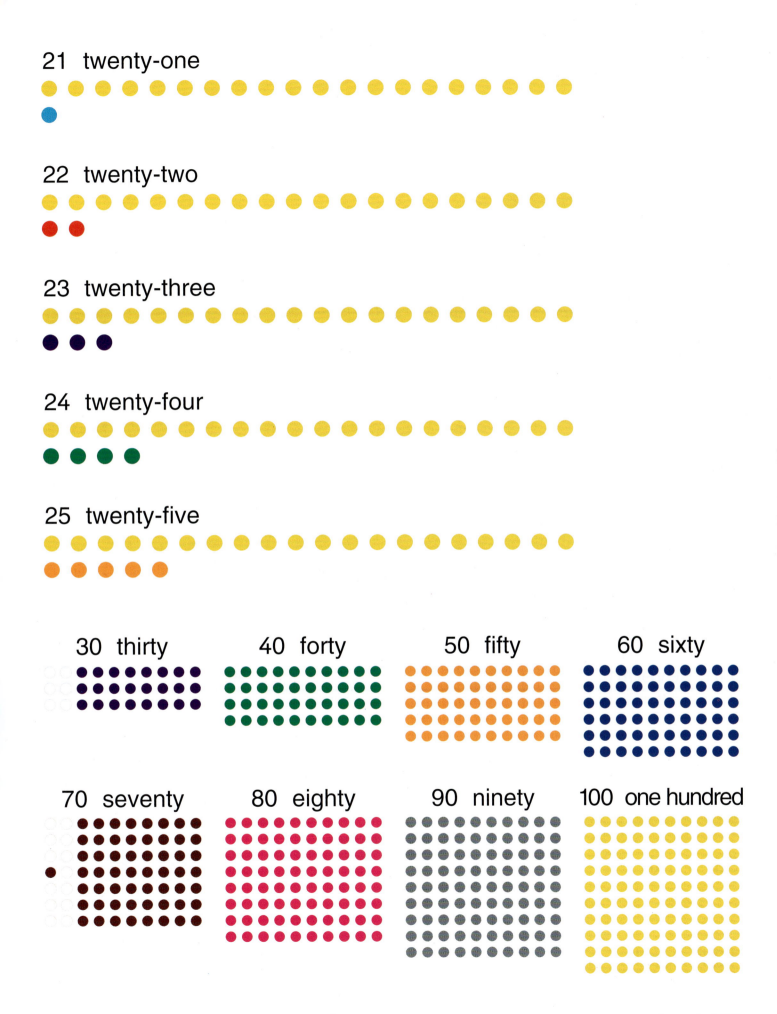

21 twenty-one

22 twenty-two

23 twenty-three

24 twenty-four

25 twenty-five

30 thirty

40 forty

50 fifty

60 sixty

70 seventy

80 eighty

90 ninety

100 one hundred

Ordinal Numbers

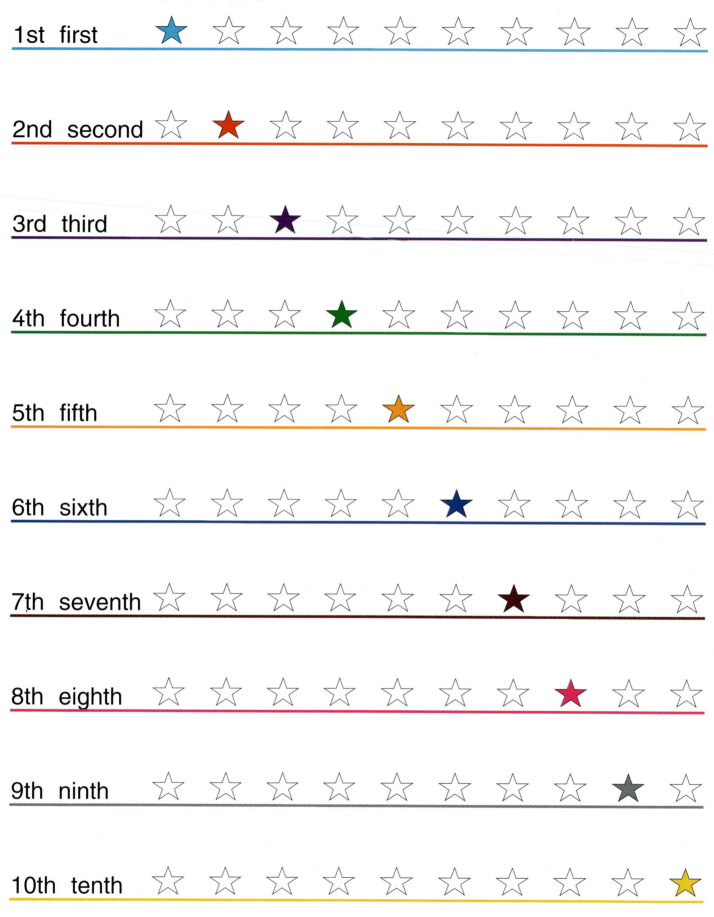

1st first

2nd second

3rd third

4th fourth

5th fifth

6th sixth

7th seventh

8th eighth

9th ninth

10th tenth

Colors

red

blue

yellow

green

purple

orange

brown

pink

gray

tan

black

white

Shapes

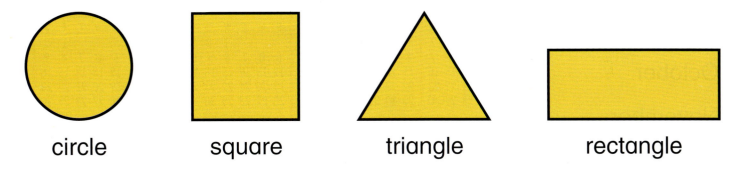

circle

square

triangle

rectangle

Days of the Week

Sunday

Monday

Tuesday

Wednesday

Thursday

Friday

Saturday

Sunday	Monday	Tuesday	Wednesday	Thursday	Friday	Saturday
		1	2	3	4	5
6	7	8	9	10	11	12
13	14	15	16	17	18	19

Months of the Year

January

February

March

April

May

June

July

August

September

October

November

December

January						
S	M	T	W	T	F	S
						1
2	3	4	5	6	7	8
9	10	11	12	13	14	15
16	17	18	19	20	21	22
23	24	25	26	27	28	29
30	31					

February						
S	M	T	W	T	F	S
		1	2	3	4	5
6	7	8	9	10	11	12
13	14	15	16	17	18	19
20	21	22	23	24	25	26
27	28	29				

March						
S	M	T	W	T	F	S
			1	2	3	4
5	6	7	8	9	10	11
12	13	14	15	16	17	18
19	20	21	22	23	24	25
26	27	28	29	30	31	

April						
S	M	T	W	T	F	S
						1
2	3	4	5	6	7	8
9	10	11	12	13	14	15
16	17	18	19	20	21	22
23	24	25	26	27	28	29
30						

May						
S	M	T	W	T	F	S
	1	2	3	4	5	6
7	8	9	10	11	12	13
14	15	16	17	18	19	20
21	22	23	24	25	26	27
28	29	30	31			

June						
S	M	T	W	T	F	S
				1	2	3
4	5	6	7	8	9	10
11	12	13	14	15	16	17
18	19	20	21	22	23	24
25	26	27	28	29	30	

July						
S	M	T	W	T	F	S
						1
2	3	4	5	6	7	8
9	10	11	12	13	14	15
16	17	18	19	20	21	22
23	24	25	26	27	28	29
30	31					

August						
S	M	T	W	T	F	S
		1	2	3	4	5
6	7	8	9	10	11	12
13	14	15	16	17	18	19
20	21	22	23	24	25	26
27	28	29	30	31		

September						
S	M	T	W	T	F	S
					1	2
3	4	5	6	7	8	9
10	11	12	13	14	15	16
17	18	19	20	21	22	23
24	25	26	27	28	29	30

October						
S	M	T	W	T	F	S
1	2	3	4	5	6	7
8	9	10	11	12	13	14
15	16	17	18	19	20	21
22	23	24	25	26	27	28
29	30	31				

November						
S	M	T	W	T	F	S
			1	2	3	4
5	6	7	8	9	10	11
12	13	14	15	16	17	18
19	20	21	22	23	24	25
26	27	28	29	30		

December						
S	M	T	W	T	F	S
					1	2
3	4	5	6	7	8	9
10	11	12	13	14	15	16
17	18	19	20	21	22	23
24	25	26	27	28	29	30
31						

Time

5:00

5 pm

five o'clock

5:15

five fifteen

a quarter past five

5:30

five thirty

half past five

5:45

five forty-five

a quarter to six

Words

Words shown in red are in illustrations only. Words in black are in illustrations and text.

sister 4
sit 21
skates 110
skeleton 29
skiing 115
skin 7
skip 33
skirt 17
skull 29
sky 116
skyscrapers 67
sled 114
sleep 13
sleeping bag 90
slide 36
slippers 14-15
smile 31
smoke 72
smoke detector 73
smokestack 66
snack bar 62
snail 85
snakes 98
sneakers 16
sneeze 39
snorkel 86
snow 114
snowball 114
snowdrift 114-115
snowflakes 114
snowman 114
snowplow 114-115
soap 15
soccer 113
socks 16
soda 63
sofa 12
soil 108
Solar System 119
sore throat 38
soup 59
South America 8
space 118
spaceship 119
spider 92
spine 29
spoon 19
sports store 43
spots 103
spout 86
spray 51
spring 106
sprout 108
spurs 94-95
squirrel 107
stand 21
stars 116
statue 68-69
steel drum 68-69
steering wheel 20-21
Stegosaurus 97
stem 109
steps 69
stereo 60
stethoscope 50
sting 92-93
stir 79

stockings 16-17
stomach 28
stomachache 38
stones 84
stop sign 20-21
stores 42-43, 56-57
stove 12
stove 18-19
straight 7
straw 34-35
street 10, 68
street 42-43
street cleaner 67
stretch 32-33
stretcher 52
stripes 103
student 22
stuffed animal 16-17
subway 67
suit 16-17
summer 110
The Sun 118
sun 108-109
sunblock 82
sunburn 82
sunflowers 108-109
sunglasses 82-83
sunrise 90
sunset 74
sunshine 108
supermarket 54
surfboard 83
surprised 30
sushi 35
swan 110-111
sweater 16
sweatshirt 17
sweep 112-113
swim 83
swing 36

T

T-shirt 17
table 12
tablecloth 78
tablets 51
taco 34
tail 99
talk 61
tall 67
taxi 42
taxi 66-67
tea 78-79
teacher 22
teapot 78-79
teeth 6
telephone 10
telescope 117
television 60
temperature 38-39
tennis 110
tent 76-77
tent 90
tentacles 87
theater 69
thermometer 38
thermometer 50-51

think 27
through 32
throw 37
thumb 28-29
thunder 110-111
thunderstorm 111
ticks 93
ticket 76
ticket booth 62-63
tide pool 84
tie 30-31
tiger 98
tired 30
tissues 38
toaster 18-19
toe 29
toilet 15
toilet paper 15
tomato 58
tongue depressors
    38-39
tooth 6
toothbrush 14
toothpaste 15
top 42-43
towel 15
tower 24-25
town 56
toys 44
toy store 43
tractor 88
traffic 42
traffic light 42
traffic light 60-67
train 44
trapeze 76
tray 34
tree 11
triangle 41
Triceratops 96
trombone 40-41, 60-61
trowel 106-107
truck 42
trumpet 40
trunk 99
tuba 40
tugboat 75
tumble 33
turtle 46
turtle 86-87
tusk 98-99
TV 12-13, 60-61
twins 4-5
Tyrannosaurus Rex 97

U

umbrella 82-83
umbrella 109
uncle 5
under 32, 86
underground 108-109
underwear 16
United States 8-9, 80-81
upside-down 36-37
Uranus 119
USA 80
USA 8-9, 80-81

V

vase 12-13, 60-61
vegetables 54-55
Venus 118
videotape 49
violin 40
volcano 97

W

waiter 79
waiting room 51, 52
walk 23
walker 53
warehouse 75
warmups 32-33
wash 13
washcloth 14-15
wastebasket 27
watch 61
water 14
water (verb) 107
water hole 102-103
waterfall 90
watering can 106-107
waterskiing 110
wave (noun) 82
wave (verb) 74-75,
    76-77
wear 16
web 92
weigh 50-51
wetlands 81
whale 86
wheel 4-5, 20-21
wheelbarrow 112
wheelchair 53
wheelchair 4-5, 48-49,
    106-107
whistle 36-37, 82-83
wichity grubs 100
wind 111
window 11
wings 101
winter 114
wire 71
wok 78-79
woman 4-5
wombat 101
wood 70-71
woodpecker 113
woods 91
world 8
worried 31
wrapping paper 64
wrist 29
write 27

X

X ray 53

y

yard 11
yawn 31

Z

zebra 102
zoo 98

Verbs

Topic 6: Good morning!
brush
cook
eat
get dressed
sleep
wash

Topic 10: Here comes the school bus!
lean
push
sit
stand

Topic 11: Time for school!
ride
walk

Topic 12: What are you making?
build
cut
listen
look
paint

Topic 13: Where's my homework?
draw
read
think
write

Topic 15: What's new in the hall?
cry
frown
laugh
smile
yawn

Topic 16: Gym time!
crawl
hop
jump
skip
tumble

Topic 18: Let's play!
bounce
catch
climb
fall
kick
run
throw

Topic 19: What's the matter?
cough
lie down
sneeze

Topic 20: Music!
beat
blow
clap
sing

Topic 24: Let's go to the library!
check out
return

Topic 30: Nice evening!
help
play
practice
rest
talk
watch

Topic 39: Great restaurant!
chop
pour
serve
stir

Topic 41: Beach day
dive
float
swim

Topic 44: Working on the farm
drive
feed
milk
pick

Subjects

Animals

Topic 23: Can we have a pet?
bird
cat
dog
fish
kitten
mouse
puppy
turtle

Topic 41: Beach day
seagull

Topic 42: We found a tide pool!
clams
crabs
duck
geese
goose
minnows
pelican
snail

Topic 43: What's under the sea?
dolphin
jellyfish
octopus
sea horse
shark
whale

Topic 44: Working on the farm
cow
hen
pig
rooster
sheep

Topic 45: Camping out
bear
deer
frog

Topic 46: Bugs!
ant
bee
butterfly
caterpillar
firefly
mosquito
spider
tick

Topic 47: Ranch in the desert
buffalo
coyote
horse
lizard

prairie dog
rattlesnake
scorpion

Topic 48: Dinosaur days
dinosaurs
Diplodocus
Oviraptor
Pterosaur
Stegosaurus
Triceratops
Tyrannosaurus Rex

Topic 49: Who lives in the zoo?
apes
elephant
lion
monkeys
peacock
snakes
tiger

Topic 50: I'm in Australia!
dingo
emu
joey
kangaroo
koala
kookaburra
parrot
wichity grubs
wombat

Topic 51: I'm in Africa!
baboon
chimpanzee
flamingo
gazelle
giraffe
gorilla
hippopotamus
leopard
zebra

Topic 52: I'm in Asia!
camel
cobra
crocodile
egret
orangutan
panda
rhinoceros

Topic 53: Spring is here!
rabbit
raccoon
robin
squirrel

Topic 56: Windy fall
woodpecker